Praise for *Fire on a Circle*

"Kim Ward's poems wrestle fiercely with life forces, some massive as a hurricane, and some that surge from and through a single tender soul. Her poems are deeply embodied, spoken by a passionate 'I' engaged with a tantalizing 'you' that is sometimes human, sometimes more. As in 'mouth of time, moth of words…' spiritual fires may dance within wordplay but they leap out as searing embers. 'God takes the tongue and roots it elsewhere, lights your bones with eternal flame…And the blessings burn.'"

—Judith Chalmer, author of *Minnow*

"Ward moves seamlessly from one emotionally authentic poem to another, each of which celebrates in its own way the states of being known as love and survival. These poems demonstrate a clear sense of unapologetic presence, of herself, but also of an 'other,' a love interest, or a muse she invokes. Along the winding roads of verse she takes occasional and welcome refuge in poetic prose, and, midway through the book, gives the reader solace in a collection of informal odes to the Germanic Runes. In one of these…we find ourselves on our own journey in the circle of life…She stokes the fire that blazes the reader through a series of personal and communal stories of devastation, truthfully told, without even a hint of sentimentalism."

—Buffy Aakaash, author of *Untangling the Knots*

"*Fire on a Circle* brings a fresh voice to Vermont's poetic landscape. The poems in this volume reveal important truths about human interactions with nature, with each other, and with other beings on the planet. The image invoked by the title conveys a warning and the closely observed depictions of life in Vermont fly in the face of the storybook setting promoted by the tourist industry. Ward renders with searing clarity the danger lurking behind the postcard representations of the Green Mountain State. The midsection of the book employs the time-honored configuration of the rune to send contemporary dispatches. Here and elsewhere, the stark urgency of the poems is leavened by suggestions of hope and possibility. This work will resonate long after readers' initial reading. I recommend that you pick it up now."

—Linda Quinlan, author of *Chelsea Creek*, winner of the Wicked Women Poetry Award sponsored by BrickHouse Books

"Kim Ward's debut collection will stir you up with lines like, 'Although I thought I was / A woman, turned out I was / A flea on the back of a cow.' You'll also be curious—how does one mind have all of these different ideas in its head, and how is it that they all fit together cohesively in one book? Ward gifts us poetry about growing up in rural Vermont as well as her observations of the mundane and the tragic. She writes provocatively about sexuality and womanhood, and even includes a section about 'Green Mountain Runes.' Poems like 'Vermont Calendar' will grab you by the guts and haunt you. Others will make you laugh really hard. Overall, this book is well-crafted and unpredictable with intriguing line breaks and vast subject matter that somehow all make sense together."

—Robyn Joy, president of the Poetry Society of Vermont

Fire on a Circle

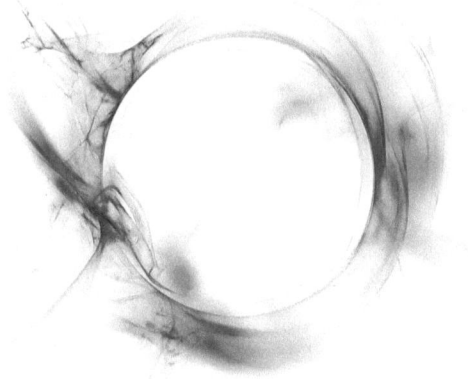

poems by

Kim Ward

Montpelier, VT

Fire on a Circle copyright 2024 ©Kim Ward
All Rights Reserved.
Release Date: April 23, 2024

Printed in the USA.

Published by Rootstock Publishing
an imprint of Ziggy Media LLC
Montpelier, Vermont 05602
info@rootstockpublishing.com
www.rootstockpublishing.com

Paperback ISBN: 978-1-57869-114-2
Library of Congress Number: 2024933374
eBook ISBN: 978-1-57869-115-9

Cover and book design by Eddie Vincent, ENC Graphic Services.

Author photo by Emma K. Dale.

For permissions or to schedule a poetry reading or workshop, contact the author at kimwardvermont@gmail.com.

I'd like to dedicate this collection to my mother, who taught me to love the written word, and my family, both biological and found. You keep me honest, most of the time.

Contents

I: Pursuit

Movement in D Minor 3
The Way We See the World 4
Go Still. 5
Surviving 6
Suddenly 7
Mistaking Myself for Invisible 8
Your Turn 9
The Vision. 10
Psychosomatic Death Knell. 11
Dowsing the Sacred Spot 13
Solitary. 14
Recovering Wife Speaks 15
Compass 16
The People Beneath the Cathedrals. 17
Spring Fish 19

II: Green Mountain Runes

Dried Ghost 23
Fehu 24
Uruz 25
Thurisaz 26
Ansuz 27
Raido 28
Kenaz 29
Gebo. 30
Wunjo. 31
Hagalaz. 32
Nauthiz 33
Isa 34
Jera 35

Green Mountain Runes...36
Dagaz...37

III: Fire

Hurricane in Vermont..41
Angel in the Fire..42
Harvest Time...44
Fever..45
Becoming the Sound of Bees................................46
What Is Vital...47
Even Now..48
This Morning's Thanks..49
Remote Control..50
Still Life with Phone..51
The Salt of Infancy..52
Eve + Testosterone = Adam..................................53
Vermont Calendar...54
No One Has Ever Believed....................................56
Disaster Porn Postcard I.......................................57
Disaster Porn Postcard II......................................58
Eating at the Chinese Buffet.................................59
Although...61
I Can Be...62

Acknowledgments...64

I

Pursuit

Movement in D Minor

It's only a dark stage, a bright circle clinging
To her yellow skirt, gray words upon her palms.

It's only a twisting body. Knives of light
Slice out and away from her small frame.

It's only one short step out of that safety
Where she sways to the chanting of the unseen crowd.

She leaps off the wooden cliff into the darkness,
Yellow skirt lifted above her head like a leaf storm.

The Way We See the World

The way we see the world crumbles
Into new country
The moment we dance outside of the circle.

The way you move entices me out,
Leaves me dreaming
We are lovers.

Do you know the desert inside of me?

See yourself become the great breath let out upon the sand,
The large crack running through the belly
Of my world.

I put my hand to your cheek,
Which dissolves
Into black night's brow,
Into lightning
traveling a warrior queen's skin.

New skies open up in my ribs
Until I cannot breathe.

You are the beating wing of tenderness,
Country of origin unknown,
Beauty unmistakable.

Go Still

Autumn air seeps into your summerhouse.
You go still inside
And feel the swirl of stars buoy you.

You go still, and deep, and
Let the incision be the path,
Let the slow, solid pump of that muscle–
The deep heart–
Carry you through.

What courses in my veins
Is poison and eternal life,
It's gamma ray and goddess shine

I forget that among the tumult of the day until

Autumn air seeps into my summerhouse,
And I go still and feel the swirl of stars buoy me.

SURVIVING

The world exists inside
Intestines of burned silk,
Filled with hot sand that sifts and sighs.

Tonight the moon, full and bloated
With her own history, beckons me from bed
And I sacrifice myself
Over chair, hang like broken meat
Hoping this nest
Of angry locusts will burst forth
From my ribs
And fly into her face.

The hours are an ax against my body.

I stake myself out
On the ocean of blue rug where
I wait for schools of fish to gnaw me clean.

Suddenly

I throw myself into the bright air of your presence.
Air sticking in lungs,
Passion held under trepidation's palm.

I let you slip into the darkness knowing
I wanted to let myself become the night air,

To wrap you tight against me,
Throw caution to the dogs like a bone just to kiss your cheek.

I touched the tingling spot on my skin until suddenly
It was day
Sun
An empty room
And nowhere in sight is your glorious presence.

Mistaking Myself for Invisible

It's been so long since anyone called me by name
Even I have forgotten.
I wake to a full moon careening overhead
Like a loosed cart on a steep hill
And realize even my dead lovers did not see past
        my plump flesh to the deep crevice
That holds my heart.

In the walled city, the wild men flocked to me,
A river of hummingbirds
Exposing the delicate undersides of their throats,
Dipping into my nectar
Again, and again to rejuvenate themselves.

Now the wide world has taken them,
Scattered their bones and dried their flesh.
The city stands empty, gates flung wide.

There is only the blank stone wall and the sunset burning through it.

My soft weeping mingles with the sibilant echo
        of a whispered name
I may never remember.

Your Turn

It's a hard rock surrounds me.
I cut it myself, eons of work.

I slide downward, ever aware
As the balm of silence grows,

While you hang above,
Lean precariously
Into my deep well.

Your voice knocks the slippery walls.
"Don't worry, I'll be here when you come up."

The encircling breeze turns your hair
Into a torrent of wings.

The Vision

There was going to be a fire.
I saw it.
The bookcase was a flame
Burning through the dark,
Words spitting outward like stars.

When I got home it was over.
The kitchen window gaped blackly.
It made me shiver to think
How close I'd been to death.

While picking through bedroom ashes,
The night came back to me.

We'd tried to rub loneliness from our bodies.
Your drunkenness was full of new shyness,
My fear of entanglement, a raw river
That parted the flames between us until

I became a lone flame, whispering,
Became
A dark warmth, a
Space at the center
Of your eye, a wing in the sternum
Of a woman,
A word I could not hear,
And the word fit itself
Inside the cry of an owl
That beat its wings
Against me until
You spoke,
Your tongue sending forth rivers of truth that,
Finally, did not burn the darkness,
But scattered it like stars.

Psychosomatic Death Knell

It's a banging in the sternum
Like a shark 'no'ing, knowing,
Gnawing at its prey.
The thrashing about we consider malevolent,
When, really, they're only messy eaters,
Unable, except in the shaking
Of the tail, like a dog to its master,
To rip open the flesh
And finally dine.

It's the staccato pluck in the veins,
Like the worry sharks must be gnawing,
'Nah'ing away at,
denying their need for fleshy feasts
So filled, in the moments
Before winter with awe
For the coming famine.
As they think to themselves,
"I can survive this.
I can survive on this until spring, this
One fatty seal, these five hundred pounds of blubber...
I CAN survive..."

That's what it is that
Starts me up, out of the
Water of sleep to look
Around and I wonder,

Stubbornly adhere to
The thought of 'no.'

No 'no'ing, knowing, no
Gnawing at me tonight, Death,
No silent quelling of the quick jerk awake,

The joke of fear, the
Junk of the unknown populating my dreams.

I've got more
To do tomorrow and I
Will not succumb
To your bad table manners,
Not tonight.

Dowsing the Sacred Spot

Rivers of energy race the distances between temples, cathedrals, small mounds of carefully chosen stones all over the world.

"Ley lines" you tell me, great veins of earth blood, spirits burrowing.

Today, we seek them out, pace by pace, avoiding the noxious, dark waters of life, the balls of anger beneath Mother Earth's belly.

All evening, I watched you stride the perimeter of our property, crisscross, like the frantic needle of a damaged compass, until you have cut the border of good karma like a quilt. Plunging the odd stick into dry dirt, you mark the invisible tent of Feng Shui under which we will camp this night. In the morning we'll begin the building of our own temple.

When you finally turn to me, beaming, "This is a strong spot, a good one. Three veins intersect here!" Your hand trembles as you point at the hill.

I smile, snuggle into the hollow knoll of your throat and whisper,

"Good. Lay me down on that intersection." I want to feel the telegraphic pulse all the way from Avebury as it creeps in under my scalp—slides down my spine like a ghost life, taking root in the smallest bones—then ride this river of Earth-blood all the way to that sacred spot.

Solitary

My single body will not multiply.
(It will die, crumble, feed the roots
Under which it sleeps.)

But perhaps a century later
I'll return as the owl or the starfish,
Become the solitary note in the dark,
The *Gloria*s sung in the rafters of some
Distant colony on the moon,

Or out of some undersea house,
Climb the shore
To my long dead garden
And plant myself in the fresh soil,
One blessed seed
To continue on the winds.

Recovering Wife Speaks

Hurry.
Close the gap between
Betrothal and denial,
Between passion and
Understanding
Why my wings did not beat
Once in thirty years of living.

Last night, I dreamt
A great turtle was running
With me on its back.
Proofreading the desert
It insisted we were on a mission

We met a woman with a wild red mane.
She fed me sweet apples.
Her lover, confusing women with eagles,
Had chased her out with a shotgun
In the middle of the night.

We proofread the desert together.
The turtle gave up its shell for us
And we swam in its bowl of ocean.
She was laughing water
And I was in the driver's seat,
        My smile bordering on cool
      Until I saw her slender hand poise to touch
     The horrific past before me,
  And awoke

Alone.

Compass

Devise for me the way by which
We might point toward
True north.
Pull the brass arms
From my stark face
And let north
Move closer to home.
Do not remove the card
From the mariner's compass
That floats in the underbelly of the world.
Instead, follow the comet as it
    Circumscribes the cool stone
        Of my city's wall,
            That pure device
            I have crafted
              To hold myself
              Accountable
            For each moment
        Traveled through
The 32 points of your days.
Fly between the Seven Sisters,
Kiss the moon and
Claim kin to kings
Who once thought
The Earth a turtle's back
The comet, a chariot for gods,
The circumscribed space
Within the narrow confines of these city walls
The world,
While I only pace my tiny brass pivot,
Arms flung wide in search of the tip
Of the sky, hoping to somehow touch
The freedom of your flight from where
I am fixed to the moss ridden stone
Of this city's walls.

The People Beneath the Cathedrals

i.

The dust down here never settles, though it is very dense, laden with soot. Shadows, when filtered through stained glass, run red with desire. These stones are heavy. We want to push them off, a passion we feel with each turn of the page. Tao, Talmud, Koran, Bible, all are scattered like bone peelings on the floor, their blanket of onion sheets does nothing to warm this shadowy mountain kirk. These memories are as light as night skies, as sharp as solar winds. They diffuse when shoved through the ancient carved sun-holes above our pale faces. When pushed up by our crumbling fingers, into the sooty air, these visions run like a handful of desert rats for the dark holes in the cracked mosaic of this mosque floor.

ii.

We have been the pull of the masses, refused to remember the faces, debated who would be king, lamb, lion, what this winter is that still suffocates our frail limbs.

We have watched, each time, the destruction of the temple, the sacrifice of the innocent, until all questions blended together in the morning light into one, repeated ceremony, one question.

What if he does not hold his wrists together? The blood will continue to spew forth from the holes. Even now, the crowds suck in cold morning air, let out a hum. It becomes one, agitated shahada that hovers like a river of hummingbirds. The dawn splinters into a kaleidoscope of winged suns to surround our faces.

"When will she speak to us?" We have asked in one large voice, as we pushed yet another initiate forward through the nets, another sacrifice, and always the sun was rising just opposite the full moon, the hand shook just before the throat was slit.

iii.

"Beneath" is not so bad. Beneath the sky, beneath
The planets, beneath the wet wool of the crowds.

Beneath this chapel of glass, we hear
The chiming of souls as they leave their shells
In the open ceiling and ascend.

Bumping the side of this tiny tomb,
They fling themselves up, out
Into a feather-splinter of moons
Above this cathedral.

Spring Fish

The fishermen's flames are bells
In the water. In crackle and
Spark, fire punctuates the silence.
The fish swim into the glint
Of hooks and steel, drift up
Toward the torches.

The deep caverns return the call
Through the wet fence of the river.
The rhythm resonates. It strikes
The air, unfurling a helix that
Climbs the wind and
Heads into
The sky.

Then, the spring fish approach,
Flick tails faster,
Hard rudders frantic,
In a spinning leap,
Arch their backs and catch
Themselves
On the searing metal of the universe.

Each twist leaves less oxygen.
Spotty vision fails. Skulls
Vibrate. The stars go out and
Suddenly the fish are Pisces, each scale
Becoming star, each vertebra, fire.

Flying through the center of
A cosmic string, untangling time,
They twist the knots
Tighter until the stars expand.
The galaxy dances outward.

II

Green Mountain Runes

Dried Ghost

A small cave, smoke
On the water, an empty
Longboat once filled with
Settlers.

The rune[1] secrets itself
Inside her chest.

The men gather,
Trumpeting for war.

Hunting dogs sniff
The carving knife.
A dried ghost curls
under her tongue—
Its leaf of death
Dislodging teeth,
Waiting to spring into fruition
On the end of the spear
And the rune
She carves bloody-handed.

---

1   In Old German, Rune meant "mystery" or "secret." The symbols themselves were both magical and alphabetical.

Fehu

Fehu[2], fussy calf, short pink tongue questing,
Fehu, prosperity, your cattle are huddle in the field,
Fehu, that fuzzy-at-the-horn-root calf.
You know if you come close to the fence
I'll offer my hand as a sloppy sacrifice,
Just to feel your slick tongue seeking.
Look upon me, Fehu, with your dark eyes. The fields
Are still wet with dew, and my head is full of dreams.

---

2 Fehu: Common Germanic Rune for "prosperity." Literally, it meant "cattle."

Uruz

Uruz[3], urchin in the rock with eyes that know.
Uruz, Wild Bull's thunder on tin roof in rain.
Strength takes you up the green mountains,
Locks you in battle with the hunter and
Even if you perish, you do so with
The grace of a dance across the
Mountainside and your blood returns
To good Earth, strengthening those who come after.

---

3   Uruz: Common Germanic Rune for "strength" and also for "aurochs," a now extinct bull which was strong and hard to hunt.

THURISAZ

Thurisaz[4], Giant, I hear your steps in the forest of dawn.
Thurisaz, thorn that pricks my rib with glee.
Thurisaz, transformation of the very flesh inside of me.
Transformation happens when the thorn pricks the thumb,
Transformation, that sticky seed of the giant,
Transformation, the thrice cursed bird.
And the wind blows and the thunder rocks
As you move into night, into wings of the bird and,
When the crow cries three times, I know it is you.

---

4   Thurisaz: Common Germanic Rune for "thorn" and used in threes for spells of transformation.

Ansuz

Ansuz[5], God, mouth of time,
Moth of words, wisdom of the Wyrd.
Inside that hole, we part, grandmother.
God takes the tongue and roots it elsewhere, lights your bones
With eternal flame, sets them deep beneath my own skin
And the blessings burn. Goddess
slips her tongue over my bones,
Drills the cipher to my life deeply against hip and shin,
Breast and skull, becomes the cursed bird and flees.

---

5   Ansuz: Common Germanic Rune for "Breath of God." Ansuz was an Aesir god.

Raido

Raido[6], wheel of days crushes a month of thunder beneath its heel.
The journey is pleasure, while the world is a flame I follow.
I dip myself in the waters of the rains, live
Off of the land, and the land I travel is strange.
Give me the hand you once held out, Raido, let my horse slow
Only when it is at the end of our trail, so that I may know to stop.
The pursuit is fire on a circle, water anointing my bare head,
And the clear aster of a new-moon sky blazing blackly above.

---

6   Raido: Common Germanic Rune for "journey on horseback."

Kenaz

Kenaz[7], torch from within. I feel your heat fill me.
Sickness is my marrow, until I learn to tame the molten river.
Kenaz, you left me for dead on your doorstep. How could I have
Let myself fall beneath your spell? When did I blossom with this fever?
The sand of your desert temple washes my skull clean with
Passion, stuff of desert winds. Carrying no way to slake my thirst,
It forces me northward, and I go forth, riding the wind, tearing up the land until
finally, I come to the black earth, fertile with clarity.

---

7   Kenaz: Common Germanic Rune for "fire," "fever from within," or "poison."

Gebo

Gebo[8], Gift, you came adorned as no other,
Flesh of my flesh, heart of my heart, you spring from the center.
Gebo, Gyfu, you are crossed through the wet meat of my muscle
So that each time I flinch, I feel you hollowing me out
And when the crossroads of my sacrifice blaze
On the frozen lake before me,
The two limbs of blood-red wood drop away.
The pain is gone, but the holes remain.

---

8   Gebo (Old Germanic) or Gyfu (Anglo-Saxon) meant both "gift" and "contract," especially of a close relationship type (such as weddings).

Wunjo

Wunjo[9], bliss, covers my face,
Like the shawl at birth, the
Curtain through which I see.
Comfort in the frozen winds,
Water through my dry throat,
Hearth red with heat.
You, who leave me ecstatic,
Can rage, unchecked, as any other.

---

9   Wunjo: Common Germanic Rune meaning "bliss," "joy," or "ecstasy."

HAGALAZ

Hagalaz[10], Hail, Hagal, my queen
You ride the skies hard, each storm a piece of art,
The matrix of those hearts known only to you.
Chaos is your face, destruction your belly,
And underneath your bare callused feet, the frozen flesh of us all.
I stand firm, hold fast as you swoop through me,
Cold clarifies each crack in my spirit,
Wind blows all tangles from my mind
If I weather you, I weather the world before time.

---

10 Hagalaz: Common Germanic Rune representing the goddess Hagal, "hail," "destruction," or "chaos."

Nauthiz

Nauthiz[11], need,
Greedy little gnat full of
Vicious joy at taking.
I starve while feeding upon you.
I hold your hand and feel the bones
straining beneath thin flesh.
"Step carefully" you say, "but come to me."
Even as I swim frantically for your ship's prow,
I hear you confessing,
"I am not a bottomless basket of giving."

---

11 Nauthiz: Common Germanic Rune meaning literally "need," or "unfulfilled desire."

Isa

Isa[12], ice, gate through which a calm mind might pass.
You confirm me even as you stay
the very pump of the Earth's blood.
You slam down like a tomb.
I go quiet, hold my breath.
The trees clack in the sharp blue morning air.
Through you I peer into the deep sockets of my ancestors
And awake screaming, trembling, cleansed.

---

12 Isa: Common Germanic Rune for "ice" or "unknown."

Jera

Jera[13], month of Sundays, bottle of moons,
You swing with the gravity of the ages.
Harvest-end, all my labor you reward
With the sharp snap of a crisp fall morning and
The smell of glorious rot.
It is here I stand, knee deep in your day
Until rested enough to begin again.

---

13 Jera: Common Germanic Rune meaning "year," "harvest," or "reward."

Green Mountain Runes

Great Grandmother, beginning
With your bare Irish feet,
Standing on Abenaki backs,
You walked from rune to rune.
Fehu, cattle, was first. Fehu, prosperity
Which, first generation, meant sheep,
More sheep than one woman could sheer
And not go bleary eyed, and bloody handed, home.
The gold of the hills propped you up
When you walked the rolling turf
Up Snipe Ireland Road
Where the barns had yet to cure, much less sag.

Today,
I walk amidst an upturned corpse of wood and hay.
The foundation is filled with rusting scythes
And old plows and
In the field above, the graves are full.

You've moved on to Nauthiz, that greedy little rune
Full of vicious joy at taking, if you don't watch him.

I stand before your tombstone.
Below us, the highway prances
Like a nest of ticks.

The falling dark pulls yellow fool's gold from
The city on the horizon as it sparks to light.

Dagaz

She paces the room
With her eyes,
Searching for what, I cannot know.

Worry.
More than likely, she's tracking down worry with her mind,
As she has her whole life.

Single mother of three, she has worked her magic on all of us, lifting us from the dark cloud of the stormy world whenever we cried out for it.

But now, as she lies on the brink of a new magic, on the brink of

Dagaz[14], "New Day," that rune of change so sudden,
It could crack the spine in two,

It's worry she holds in her mouth,
Like a seed caught between the teeth just in time.

And as the cancer works the most devious of transformations,
She watches the birds outside in the feeder peck at seed after seed.

Perhaps she's wondering how she might
Transfer this growing, unexpected stone
From her mouth to theirs.

As I watch her, I can believe that,
Like a circus performer, she might open the window
At any minute and try it.

And in that moment,
I think the stone on her tongue

---

14 Dagaz: Common Germanic Rune for "day," "hope," "new day," or "happiness."

must have dissolved,
For she relaxes,
Sighs,
The mouth parting just a bit,
As if for a kiss
From some dark and handsome stranger.

III

Fire

Hurricane in Vermont

After the hurricane, we went out to help our neighbors.
In the dawn, the moon was just a sliver, sharp and small.

The cows beneath the collapsed barn called out like an anguished village
And were silenced with each successive blow from Daddy's shotgun.

Angel in the Fire

I am the girl you brought through the fire.
I am the singing angel in the furnace,
the voice of the hunting owl as she kills her prey.

In the beginning, I was the silent face,
all questing eyes and limbs,
my early body ready
to fling this world off.

You are Mother of mothers,
voice of the ages,
soothsayer to the aged.
Your life stretches
to the taught place
of crones become infants
and daughter become keeper.

In the stone of your hearth,
beat the hearts of tree frogs
and the wings of youth,

while I return to
the girl in the tree,
the one who lost her voice,
winter after winter,
as if the gods were stealing
her angel's fire,

so that I would
start up in bed, fever
shaking the voice out of me,

while, out in the hall, was
warm light
and the sound of your deep song
drifting.

Harvest Time

Red moon this morning.
I am walking barefoot
in puddles and find
the hogs have been killed
uphill.

FEVER

When you caught the fever, it wasn't
the doctor who told your mother what to do,
it was the whisky and water to break the fever,
the burning of the body brought down by liquid fire.
We brought you through like a horse brought through
a burning barn, while down in the yard
drifting up to us through the cold frost,
came the sound of your grandfather, praying.

Becoming the Sound of Bees
after Marc Vincenz

Becoming the sound of bees is not as easy as you would think.
First, take a cup of despondency & fold in
with a pocket full of compasses, made of afternoon light
& late summer pollen, with just a pinch of sky.
Sprinkle some loyalty to a singular woman on top.
Add a penchant for following the crowd.
Stir in a saucepan on low heat,
the kind of warmth that comes from
a late August sun at Lughnasa
Once it all comes to temperature,
simmer and wait for the sound to come.
When it does,
dive in headfirst
and hum.

What Is Vital

An expanse of space opens before me.
The taste of silence drips from my tongue.

There is an ebb and flow to being in the world,
In the morning, the struggling and climbing up,
In the evening the shrugging and falling down.

Between? I am a languid snake,
Bathing on a sun-drenched stone...

I am only just
Touching the face of me,
Fingers mapping the core of fruit,
Discovering the soft rotted ends,
Savoring the still-fresh flesh
Of what is vital...

Even Now

The memory of the razor

Tucked

Into the gutter of that magazine

And placed on the table in that grubby laundromat

Reminds me of the moment,

Age eight,

When I first learned

Words can cut…

This Morning's Thanks

Thanks,
To the man carrying the handgun in his car this morning,
To the car that flashed its lights as I came down the hill.

Thanks,
To all of us commuters rushing wearily to our destinations,
Who pulled over or stopped right in the road
To give witness.

Thanks,
To the mist on the hills dreaming of spring
That cloaked us like a loving parent's arms
From the wide-open spaces on the hill.

Thanks,
To the poor yearling that flopped in the road,
Her front legs broken by the car,
Useless to stop her terrified tumbling.

Thanks,
To the people who made the two bullets
That the young man,
Very calmly and lovingly

Put in her skull
To release her from the pain
This morning.

Thanks,
For the reminder that life is precious
And mercy rare
And rarer still
From the pinched mouth
Of a handgun.

Remote Control

Is controlling yourself from a distance
Listening to his callused hands rake
Your young breasts
As if he were the train car and you

A wild rabbit,
His passing slicing you in two,
Leaving innocence on one side,
And you on the other, while

From on high you watch
The iron stars
Strike the ground

And think about a time
When you trusted.

Still Life with Phone

Black, smoothed by generations of hands caressing its surface, heavy.
The phone sits in the center of the hallway table.
Cool to the touch.
Quiescent.
I turn the heavy metal dial,
Listen to the whirring of the gear as it returns each time.
There is a click when I lift and return the receiver, but
No buzzing at the other end.
The cable stretches, languid beneath the oak phone stand,
But connects no longer.

"The bridge is out, you'll have to spend the night," I think.
And then,

"Operator...?"

"Give me Bakersfield, 547, please."

"Get off the phone, I have to make a call!"

Still, the phone just sits there,
Holding time within its metal bowels,
The slight vibration of voices lingering
At the subatomic level. Then,

"Mother, are you there?"

And, for an instant, I think I hear you reply.

The Salt of Infancy

Began with the first inmate's death.

Curled as he was around the tongue of space
That was the cuff window
Made for hands
That somehow held his head…

"Stupid inmate." The public says. "Good riddance."

But was he 'that stupid' or that desperate in
Trying to escape the ghouls of that terrible palace?

There he lay,
Nestled, as a limp fetus in a womb of iron,
Even as he left his body and ascended,

The granulated mist of his soul flinging itself
Up over the barbed wire fence,
(Flung salt in a gale storm)

Cutting across the plains,
Headed for home.

Until he came to rest on the near empty dinner table

And was shaken into each relative's meal

Before the family even knew

The prisoner had returned,

 Salt-to-salt, Earth-to-earth,

To their empty hands.

Eve + Testosterone = Adam

"And the combination of Eve plus testosterone, would produce Adam."
—Andrea Long Chu, Females

Formula, fire, vessel, strap.
In what way did I truly first come to pass?

Eclipse, skip, turn…
                         My skin truly burns

To be let loose on the cobblestones of the city.

And if I had been thicker?
Taller?
Less pretty?

Had the formula have raged

Over a Bunsen a bit longer?
                         Then would I have surely

Been the king of my own destiny.
                               The queen left behind

In the mud pit
             in the Tin + Estrogen – Father = Trailer

Of my childhood home
                       to rot.

Vermont Calendar

I wanted to write a poem about Vermont,
But no one wants to know about my Vermont.

The streets of the trailer park flooding and freezing in winter,

The boys tripping me mercilessly as I crawled my way across that rippled expanse
of ice in a dress I'd been forced to wear to school,

The man whose trailer was the first one at the third entrance,
who chopped his wife to pieces as if he could
Fling her up and make ruby stars by which to navigate his broken heart,

Our neighbor Billy, who decided not to
Come to the bus stop on Monday
because he had a date with a tree
And a rope he could not break.

I vowed at 16—one day I would
Make my own foliage calendar and send it to *Vermont Life*
For publication…

With a January full of rusted trailers instead of collapsing bucolic barns or tractors,
and an October full of young, tortured souls falling in the bright
air in reds and black-and-blues,

And a December filled with
The panoramic picture of my neighbor, David, running
From his father's rusted truck
At midnight, cast in green, sickly night-vision,

And buyers will get a special greeting card with a microchip playing the song of his
adolescent voice calling out,

"Dad, no! Don't! Please, stop!!!"

While the growl of the engine can be heard rising and falling like a roaring fire truck,

The byline would state, "No rural poor were killed in the making of these memorabilia.

David only broke his leg that night."

No One Has Ever Believed

They were high tide
And I low

Even you,
My heart-song,
Spent too many years
Waiting in the cave
Ashore
For passion's waves
To enter

While I was swimming deep
In the Marianas
With the octopus

Oblivious to the dry shore
And your sun-warmed arms.

Disaster Porn Postcard I

Go ahead,
Take my picture,
Float downstream in your
One-man kayak and
Watch me,
My mouth Oh-ing,

A rictus cave
Akin to Munch's "The Scream,"

The chickens across the way
Screaming for release
From the tiny coup they have
Rushed into,
Childlike minds seeking a safe space,

As the waters rose tonight so

Quickly,
There was no escape.

Happy to have you visit
My street.

When you get back,
Tell them I'm here.

Disaster Porn Postcard II

I watched last night, the waters
Rise to the occasion and
Like an anxious star

Take their bow.

We took pictures, of course.
What disaster-porn reel
Is complete without a few

Paparazzi shots,
After all?
Shots,
That left out the esprit de corps,
The ones doing the heavy lifting,
The people in the parking lot
Starting their cars
For the race of a lifetime.

And when all was said and done,
Since we've got nothing more than a dark night,
A battery-lit read,
And the full-throated cry of a fire alarm,
To worry about,

What's a few days of full-bodied
Flight-or-fight
Restlessness

To the huddled masses leaving
Their streets of houses empty
And gaping blackly at the river...
Streets that were a
Throughway just minutes before?

Eating at the Chinese Buffet

I'm cognizant of four things.

i.

The General Tso's Chicken is sweet,
Not spicy hot, as it should be.

ii.

I love the Crab Rangoons
Not despite of but because
Their pillowy deep-fried cheese
Was invented just for us Americans.

iii.

I'm probably complicit
In human trafficking
Just as I was as a teen
When I'd buy those juicy
Cherry tomatoes
From my friend's "family farm,"

Though I didn't know it
Until the day I stumbled into the farmhands' house
Into a dim room with migrants sleeping
Wall-to-wall like cordwood so that…

iv.

I could take no pleasure in those August jewels
As I popped them in my mouth.
Their bursting on my tongue
No longer a manna from the gods
But now more a burst of blood vessels,
Much too salty on my tongue.

Although

Although I took myself to be
An adult, I turned out
To be a baby in an aging
Carriage of carrion bones.

Although I thought I had
Cut you free,
My foot got entangled
In your seeping soul
As it slithered out of
The last bottle you
left in my apartment.

Although I thought I was
A woman, turned out I was
A flea on the back of a cow.

Although I let my rancor go
It flew back to me
    spearing my chest,
Exploding my heart into a cloud
Of red ravens.

I Can Be...

I can be…
Pink ribbons,
Classical tutus,
Pointe shoes
And bird-folded arms.

I can be…
Pirate boots
Leather pants
Poet's shirt with billowed sleeves
And swashbuckling sword.

I can be…
Jeans and frumpy T-shirt

I can be...
Dyke boots and chained keyring.

I can be barefoot in a spring dress with daffodils in its folds.

I can be…

Acknowledgments

Thank you to Sam for support and encouragement to make this project happen, and to the following for previously publishing the following poems:

Circumference, The Poetry Anthology of Gloucester County College, Sewell, NJ: "Beneath the Cathedrals" (1994).

Birchsong: Poetry Centered in Vermont, Volume I, by Blueline Press: "Hurricane in Vermont" and "Harvest Time" (2012).

Birchsong: Poetry Centered in Vermont, Volume II, by Blueline Press: "Green Mountain Runes" and "Telling the Truth & Recipe for Honey" (2018).

Kim Ward is a poet, playwright, and visual and theater artist. She is the founder of The Vermont Playwrights Circle and received her MFA in Performance Poetry from Goddard College in 1998. Her poetic play "Angel in the Fire" received the 1999 Playwrights Showcase Award by the Vermont Actors and Theater Artists Association and was also accepted into the New Frontiers Conference in 2000. She grew up in Vermont and has lived in Montpelier for over twenty years. She teaches English at Norwich University.

 More Titles in the Rootstock Poetry Series

Indigo Hours: Healing Haiku by Nancy Stone

Lifting Stones by Doug Stanfield

Mountain Offerings by Amy Allen

PoemCity Anthology 2023 by Kellogg-Hubbard Library

PoemCity Anthology 2024 by Kellogg-Hubbard Library

Safe as Lightning by Scudder H. Parker

Stonechat by Mary Elder Jacobsen

The Lost Grip by Eva Zimet

To the Man in the Red Suit by Christina Fulton

Unleashed: Poems & Drawings by Betty Nadine Thomas

Poetry submissions are open. Learn more and submit at www.rootstockpublishing.com.